All patterns in this book may be worked with Peyote Stitch or [Brick] Stitch. I personally bead the rectangular designs with Peyote Stitch. Th[e] one I recommend Brick Stitch for is the Soaring Eagle pattern on page [ ]

Basic Brick Stitch Instructions

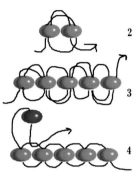

Row 1 Row one base row: Usually the middle or widest row is the base row unless indicated otherwise on the pattern. Pick up 2 beads on your needle and position them toward the end of the thread. Holding beads in place with your thumb and forefinger, run the needle through them again in same direction making a circle.

2 Pull the circle tight positioning the 2 beads side by side.

3 Continue adding more beads until you have the total you need for the base row.

4 Turn work around. Always work from left to right. For the second row, with a bead on the thread, bring the needle through the top loop that goes between the last 2 beads of the very first row.

5 Pull the bead into place. Bring the needle back up through the bead coming up through the bottom and pull it down.

6 If the thread is pulled too tight, the beadwork becomes rigid and warped. Just pull up the slack until the bead is snug. Continue to add beads as shown to the end of the row.

7 Turn and continue in the same manner for the remaining rows.

8 Weave the thread through the finished work and clip the thread close to the beads.

Joining Seams

To join a peyote stitch with a 'zipper' join, have both of your edges meet with the beads alternating on either side so they will interlock like a zipper. Take your thread through the first end bead, through the next bead that fits into the 'zipper' on the other side and continue this way, pulling on the thread every 3 or 4 stitches. Don't pull too tight or your work will warp.

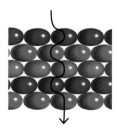

Ideas for Fringe

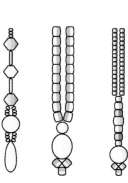
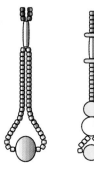

When you string the fringe, all the bead holes are facing down, so the strands of fringe will hang straight down from the bag, forming two side by side rows of thick fringe.

SUPPLIERS - Most bead stores carry an excellent assortment of beads. For special needs, ask your store to contact the following companies: **Helby Imports**, 732-969-5300, Carteret, NJ

Yellow Frog

This happy frog is a favorite because he is so graphic. A bright yellow frog lampwork bead really complements the bright yellow frog in this playful design. The rose lampwork beads accent the pink colors on the frog's back.

Stitch: Peyote or Brick   Size: Approximately 3¾" x 4⅛"   Beads Used: Delica

Begin Here - work Peyote Stitch beginning with this row. Work from left to right across the pattern.

For straps and embellishments, gather your own collection of beads, natural stones and crystals. Plan a design that makes the bag uniquely yours. Note: The bead quantities given do not include fringe and strap.

Bag by Pam Davies, St. Catherines, Ontario, Canada
Yellow Frog lampwork and Pink lampwork beads by LandS Art   landsart.com

#203 - Ceylon Lt. Yellow
127 beads

#205 - Ceylon Beige
107 beads

#207 - Op. Peach Luster
32 beads

#310 - Matte Black
1485 beads

#233 - Lined Crystal Yellow Luster
24 beads

#420 - Galvanized Pink
47 beads

#1363- Dyed Op. Peach
130 beads

#232 - Pale Yellow Pearl
91 beads

#854 - Matte Transp. Yellow AB
126 beads

#055 - Lined Pale Pink
50 beads

#085 - Lined Blue AB
32 beads

#685 - Semi Matte Silver Lined Dk. Rose
51 beads

#651 - Dyed Op. Squash
276 beads

#744 - Matte Transp. Orange
56 beads

#062 - Lined Strawberry Ice AB
18 beads

#105 - Gold Luster Transp. Dk. Red
16 beads

#106 - Transp. Pink Luster
39 beads

#129 - Pink Luster Topaz
63 beads

#296 - Lined Red Cranberry AB
16 beads

#053 - Lined Pale Yellow AB
114 beads

#297 - Lined Ruby Black
107 beads

#160 - Op. Yellow AB
555 beads

#275 - Lined Green Teal Luster
100 beads

#276 - Lined Green Teal AB
460 beads

#324 - Matte Met. Green Iris
144 beads

#327 - Matte Met. Teal Iris
326 beads

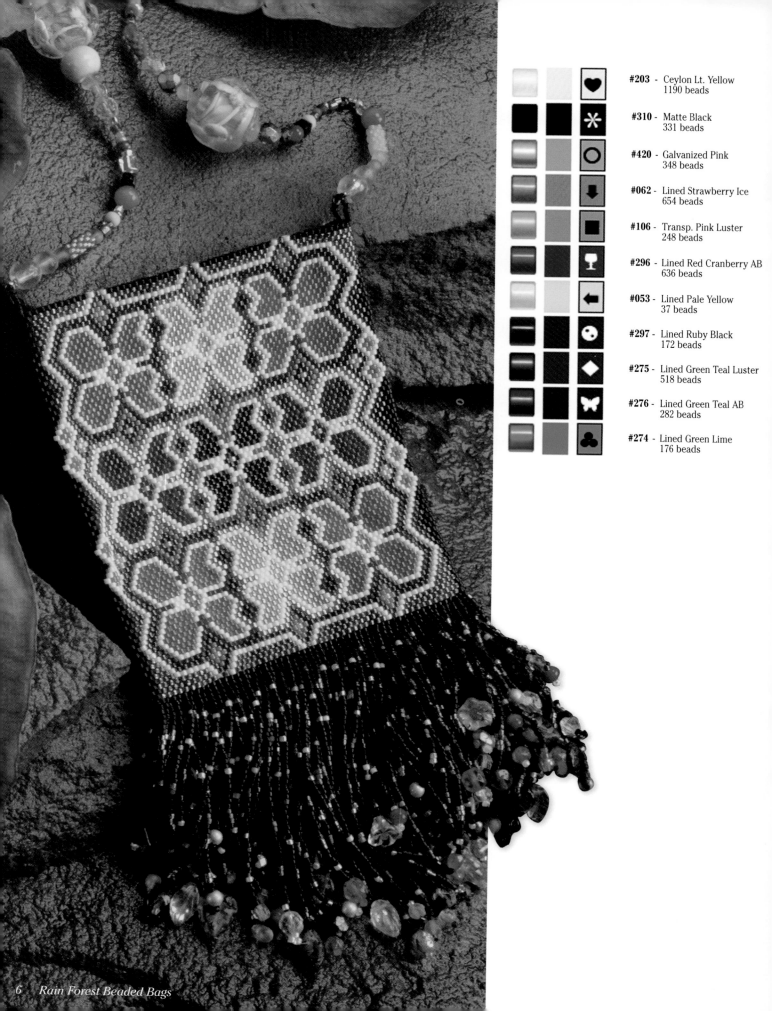

#203 - Ceylon Lt. Yellow
1190 beads

#310 - Matte Black
331 beads

#420 - Galvanized Pink
348 beads

#062 - Lined Strawberry Ice
654 beads

#106 - Transp. Pink Luster
248 beads

#296 - Lined Red Cranberry AB
636 beads

#053 - Lined Pale Yellow
37 beads

#297 - Lined Ruby Black
172 beads

#275 - Lined Green Teal Luster
518 beads

#276 - Lined Green Teal AB
282 beads

#274 - Lined Green Lime
176 beads

This rose flower geometric would make an elegant piece of wall art. Geometrics are easy to stitch and you can change your colors if desired.

Stitch: Peyote or Brick   Size: Approximately 3¾" x 4⅛"   Beads Used: Delica

Begin Here - work Peyote Stitch beginning with this row. Work from left to right across the pattern.

For straps and embellishments, gather your own collection of beads, natural stones and crystals. Plan a design that makes the bag uniquely yours. Note: The bead quantities given do not include fringe and strap.

Bag by Pam Davies, St. Catherines, Ontario, Canada
Pink lampwork beads by LandS Art   landsart.com

Raja

Feeling powerful today? Here's a design to roar about. The topaz, gold, and chocolate beads bring this magnificent tiger to life.

Stitch: Peyote or Brick   Size: Approximately 3¾" x 4⅛"   Beads Used: Delica

Begin Here - work Peyote Stitch beginning with this row. Work from left to right across the pattern.

For straps and embellishments, gather your own collection of beads, natural stones and crystals. Plan a design that makes the bag uniquely yours. Note: The bead quantities given do not include fringe and strap.

Bag by Belinda Bouffioux, Finchville, KY   Belinda719@cs.com
Glass beads by XBead   griver@zianet.com

#054 - Lined Peach AB
54 beads

#203 - Ceylon Lt. Yellow
68 beads

#205 - Ceylon Beige
52 beads

#208 - Op. Tan
23 beads

#352 - Matte Cream
144 beads

#853 - Matte Transp. Dk. Topaz AB
258 beads

#863 - Matte Transp. Shark Gray AB
36 beads

#884 - Matte Op. Chocolate AB
152 beads

#230 - 22kt. Lined Gold
113 beads

#256 - Lt. Coffee Pearl
192 beads

#052 - Lined Palest Peach AB
31 beads

#323 - Matte Met. Purple Iris
39 beads

#460 - Galvanized Rose Gold
53 beads

#325 - Matte Met. Blue Iris
58 beads

#380 - Matte Met. Green Pink
346 beads

#742 - Matte Transp. Topaz
27 beads

#242 - Gray Pearl
41 beads

#066 - Lined White AB
66 beads

#084 - Lined Lt. Seafoam
23 beads

#234 - Pale Pink Pearl
24 beads

#372 - Matte Met. Lt. Yellow Green
26 beads

#411 - Galvanized Met. Gold
79 beads

#851 - Matte Transp. Crystal AB
667 beads

#107 - Transp. Gray Iris
83 beads

#306 - Matte Dk. Gray
672 beads

#241 - Pale Lavender Pearl
64 beads

#252 - Ceylon Gray
54 beads

#660 - Dyed Op. Lavender
198 beads

#865 - Matte Transp. Dk. Chocolate AB
109 beads

#882 - Matte Op. Sharkskin AB
215 beads

#209 - Op. Pale Gray Luster
61 beads

#080 - Lined Pale Lavender AB
77 beads

#179 - Transp. Lt. Gray AB
38 beads

#373 - Matte Met. Leaf Green
122 beads

#301 - Matte Met. Blue Gray
327 beads

#863 - Matte Rainbow Transp. Gray
744 beads

#411 - Galvanized Met. Gold
930 beads

#851 - Matte Rainbow Transp. Crystal
184 beads

#306 - Matte Dk. Gray
1138 beads

#660 - Dyed Op. Lavender
546 beads

#865 - Matte Transp. Dk. Chocolate AB
240 beads

#373 - Matte Met. Leaf Green
810 beads

If you love the complex look of geometric patterns from India and Persia, you are going to love making this green and purple set of diamonds. Gold beads sharpen the image the same way backstitching makes a cross stitch image stand out.

Stitch: Peyote or Brick   Size: Approximately 3¾" x 4⅛"   Beads Used: Delica

For straps and embellishments, gather your own collection of beads, natural stones and crystals. Plan a design that makes the bag uniquely yours. Note: The bead quantities given do not include fringe and strap.

Bag by Belinda Bouffioux, Finchville, KY   Belinda719@cs.com
Glass beads by XBead   griver@zianet.com

Egret

You are walking through a rain forest. The dappled sunlight creates scattered shadows everywhere. A rustling sound captures your attention as a beautiful egret takes flight, her white feathers glistening against the dark forest leaves. Capture the experience with this amazing beadwork.

Stitch: Peyote or Brick   Size: Approximately 3¾" x 4⅛"   Beads Used: Delica

Begin Here - work Peyote Stitch beginning with this row. Work from left to right across the pattern.

For straps and embellishments, gather your own collection of beads, natural stones and crystals. Plan a design that makes the bag uniquely yours. Note: The bead quantities given do not include fringe and strap.

Bag by Roberta Dildine   bddildine@designsbydeb.com

#310 - Matte Black
1030 beads

#351 - Matte White
621 beads

#218 - Op. Lt. Blue Luster
80 beads

#239 - Lt. Aqua Pearl
219 beads

#158 - Op. Lavender AB
163 beads

#660 - Dyed Op. Lavender
137 beads

#758 - Matte Op. Lt. Lavender
80 beads

#651 - Dyed Op. Squash
83 beads

#858 - Matte Transp. Kelly Green AB
80 beads

#377 - Matte Met. Dk. Gray Blue
123 beads

#275 - Lined Green Teal Luster
153 beads

#373 - Matte Met. Leaf Green
141 beads

#788 - Dyed Matte Met. Teal
108 beads

#323 - Matte Met. Purple Iris
82 beads

#876 - Matte Op. Green AB
15 beads

#730 - Op. Periwinkle
138 beads

#055 - Lined Pale Pink
50 beads

#117 - Lavender Blue Gold Luster
58 beads

#356 - Matte Lavender
88 beads

#295 - Lined Red AB
79 beads

#430 - Galvanized Plum
92 beads

#325 - Matte Met. Blue Iris
177 beads

#233 - Lined Crystal Yellow Luster
44 beads

#176 - Transp. Sky Blue AB
95 beads

#419 - Galvanized Dk. Rose
65 beads

#744 - Matte Transp. Orange
40 beads

#077 - Lined Blue AB
314 beads

#297 - Lined Ruby Black
28 beads

#003 - Green Iris
128 beads

#276 - Lined Green Teal AB
50 beads

#877 - Matte Op. Green AB
31 beads

Sunrise
Back of Egret

The bright yellow and white in this sparkling medallion highlight the intricate design. This wonderful work of art is very attractive against a denim shirt.

Stitch: Peyote or Brick   Size: Approximately 3¾" x 4⅛"   Beads Used: Delica

Begin Here - work Peyote Stitch beginning with this row. Work from left to right across the pattern.

For straps and embellishments, gather your own collection of beads, natural stones and crystals. Plan a design that makes the bag uniquely yours. Note: The bead quantities given do not include fringe and strap.

Bag by Roberta Dildine   bddildine@designsbydeb.com

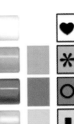

❤	**#351** -	Matte White 342 beads
✳	**#651** -	Dyed Op. Squash 332 beads
○	**#295** -	Lined Red AB 370 beads
⬇	**#233** -	Lined Crystal Yellow Luster 171 beads
■	**#744** -	Matte Transp. Orange 570 beads
♟	**#077** -	Lined Blue AB 2217 beads
⬅	**#297** -	Lined Ruby Black 590 beads

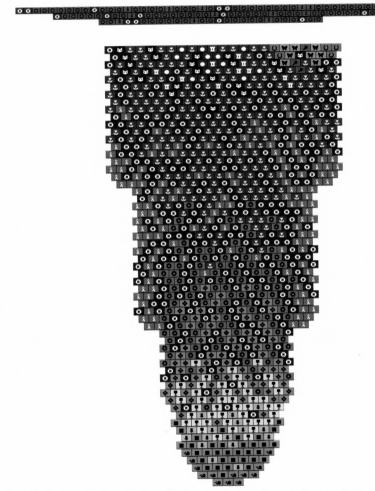

Parrot Tail of
Paulie & Pansie

*Chart for the parrot tail,
refer to colors on
pages 16 - 19.*

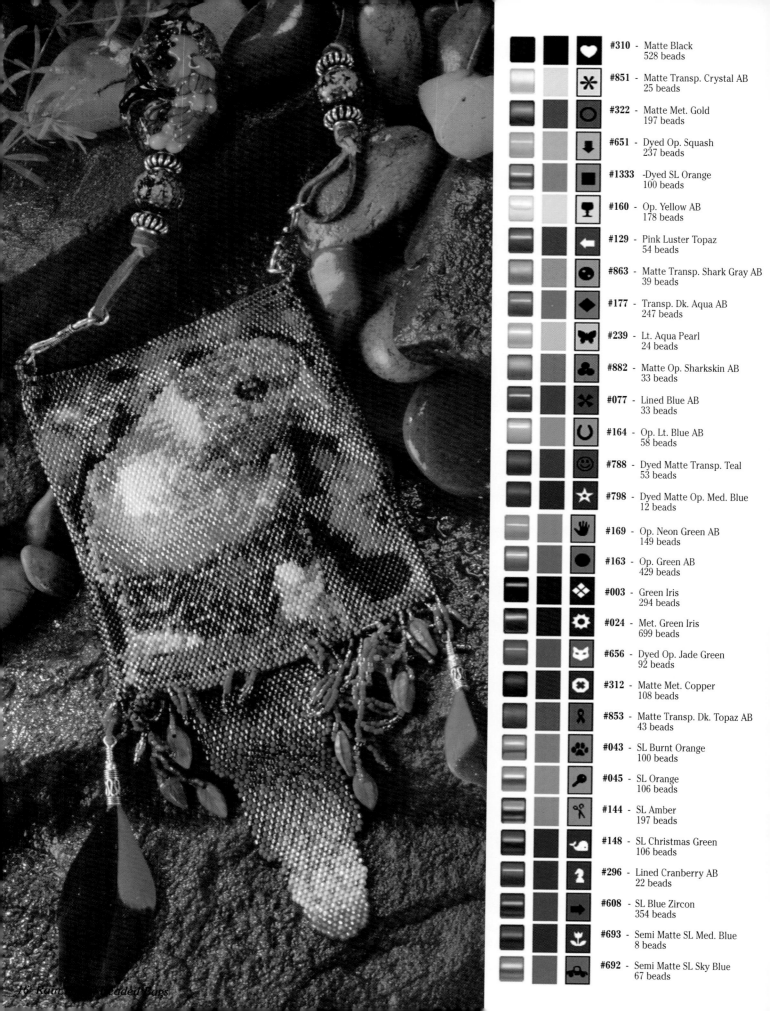

		♥	#310 - Matte Black 528 beads
		✳	#851 - Matte Transp. Crystal AB 25 beads
		⬤	#322 - Matte Met. Gold 197 beads
		⬇	#651 - Dyed Op. Squash 237 beads
		■	#1333 - Dyed SL Orange 100 beads
		♈	#160 - Op. Yellow AB 178 beads
		←	#129 - Pink Luster Topaz 54 beads
		☯	#863 - Matte Transp. Shark Gray AB 39 beads
		◆	#177 - Transp. Dk. Aqua AB 247 beads
		🦋	#239 - Lt. Aqua Pearl 24 beads
		♣	#882 - Matte Op. Sharkskin AB 33 beads
		✖	#077 - Lined Blue AB 33 beads
		⎝	#164 - Op. Lt. Blue AB 58 beads
		☺	#788 - Dyed Matte Transp. Teal 53 beads
		☆	#798 - Dyed Matte Op. Med. Blue 12 beads
		✋	#169 - Op. Neon Green AB 149 beads
		●	#163 - Op. Green AB 429 beads
		❖	#003 - Green Iris 294 beads
		⚙	#024 - Met. Green Iris 699 beads
		🐱	#656 - Dyed Op. Jade Green 92 beads
		✲	#312 - Matte Met. Copper 108 beads
		⚑	#853 - Matte Transp. Dk. Topaz AB 43 beads
		🐾	#043 - SL Burnt Orange 100 beads
		⚷	#045 - SL Orange 106 beads
		✂	#144 - SL Amber 197 beads
		🐋	#148 - SL Christmas Green 106 beads
		♘	#296 - Lined Cranberry AB 22 beads
		→	#608 - SL Blue Zircon 354 beads
		⚘	#693 - Semi Matte SL Med. Blue 8 beads
		🚗	#692 - Semi Matte SL Sky Blue 67 beads

The tail on this parrot is perfectly designed to match each bird. Paulie and Pansy would also look great on a wall hanging stitched side by side - just a couple of love birds that everyone will love! see tail pattern on page 15

Paulie
Back of Pansie

Stitch: Peyote or Brick   Size: Approximately 3¾" x 4⅛"   Beads Used: Delica

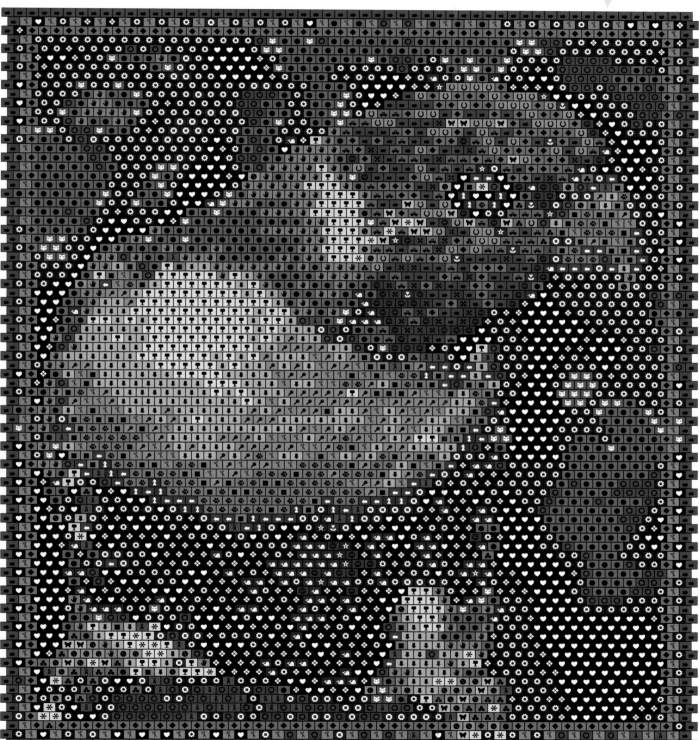

this row. Work from left to right across the pattern.

For straps and embellishments, gather your own collection of beads, natural stones and crystals. Plan a design that makes the bag uniquely yours. Note: The bead quantities given do not include fringe and strap.

Bag by Coni Vestel
Parrot lampwork beads by LandS Art   landsart.com

Pansie
Back of Paulie

No symbol of the rain forest is more well known than the parrot. This beaded example is as exotic as the real thing. The beaded tail is a perfect completion to this project. Notice the parrot lampwork bead and the feathers in the fringe. Both are perfect for this theme.

see tail pattern on page 15

Stitch: Peyote or Brick   Size: Approximately 3¾" x 4⅛"   Beads Used: Delica

•Begin Here - work Peyote Stitch beginning with this row. Work from left to right across the pattern.

For straps and embellishments, gather your own collection of beads, natural stones and crystals. Plan a design that makes the bag uniquely yours. Note: The bead quantities given do not include fringe and strap.

Bag by Coni Vestel
Parrot lampwork beads by LandS Art   landsart.com

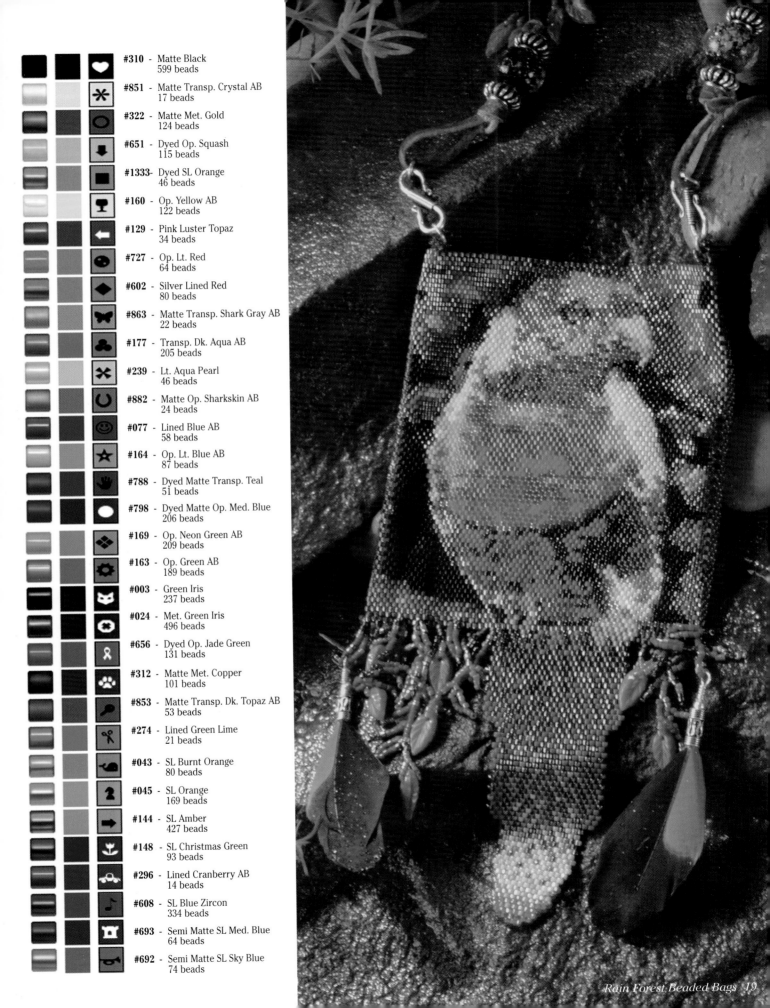

		♥	**#310** -	Matte Black 599 beads
		✳	**#851** -	Matte Transp. Crystal AB 17 beads
		◯	**#322** -	Matte Met. Gold 124 beads
		⬇	**#651** -	Dyed Op. Squash 115 beads
		■	**#1333** -	Dyed SL Orange 46 beads
		♆	**#160** -	Op. Yellow AB 122 beads
		←	**#129** -	Pink Luster Topaz 34 beads
		◉	**#727** -	Op. Lt. Red 64 beads
		◆	**#602** -	Silver Lined Red 80 beads
		🦋	**#863** -	Matte Transp. Shark Gray AB 22 beads
		♣	**#177** -	Transp. Dk. Aqua AB 205 beads
		✱	**#239** -	Lt. Aqua Pearl 46 beads
		☂	**#882** -	Matte Op. Sharkskin AB 24 beads
		☺	**#077** -	Lined Blue AB 58 beads
		☆	**#164** -	Op. Lt. Blue AB 87 beads
		✋	**#788** -	Dyed Matte Transp. Teal 51 beads
		◯	**#798** -	Dyed Matte Op. Med. Blue 206 beads
		⬧	**#169** -	Op. Neon Green AB 209 beads
		⚙	**#163** -	Op. Green AB 189 beads
		🐱	**#003** -	Green Iris 237 beads
		✪	**#024** -	Met. Green Iris 496 beads
		⚥	**#656** -	Dyed Op. Jade Green 131 beads
		🐾	**#312** -	Matte Met. Copper 101 beads
		🥄	**#853** -	Matte Transp. Dk. Topaz AB 53 beads
		✂	**#274** -	Lined Green Lime 21 beads
		🐌	**#043** -	SL Burnt Orange 80 beads
		♟	**#045** -	SL Orange 169 beads
		→	**#144** -	SL Amber 427 beads
		🌷	**#148** -	SL Christmas Green 93 beads
		🚗	**#296** -	Lined Cranberry AB 14 beads
		♪	**#608** -	SL Blue Zircon 334 beads
		🏠	**#693** -	Semi Matte SL Med. Blue 64 beads
		⛵	**#692** -	Semi Matte SL Sky Blue 74 beads

Stealth

Peyote stitch lends itself so well to creating the subtle shading essential in this life-like leopard. She should be purring at you any minute, and your friends will too when they see this marvelous work of art.

★	#373	-	Matte Met. Leaf Green	182 beads
☆	#690	-	Semi Matte SL Dk. Gray Gr	156 beads
L	#463	-	Galvanized Dk. Fuchsia	241 beads

Stitch: Peyote or Brick   Size: Approximately 3¾" x 4⅛"   Beads Used: Delica

Begin Here - work Peyote Stitch beginning with this row. Work from left to right across the pattern.

For straps and embellishments, gather your own collection of beads, natural stones and crystals. Plan a design that makes the bag uniquely yours. Note: The bead quantities given do not include fringe and strap.

Bag by Suzanne Siegel, Kalispell, MT   ssiegel@cyberport.net
Iris Glass by Iris Glass Art   irisglassart@cox.net

		♥	**#203** - Ceylon Lt. Yellow 82 beads
		✳	**#204** - Ceylon Lt. Beige 77 beads
		○	**#205** - Ceylon Beige 55 beads
		⬇	**#208** - Op. Tan 51 beads
		◼	**#352** - Matte Cream 101 beads
		♈	**#857** - Matte Transp. Lt. Amethyst AB 146 beads
		←	**#884** - Matte Op. Chocolate AB 72 beads
		☻	**#230** - 22 kt. Gold Lined 514 beads
		◆	**#321** - Matte Met. Silver 280 beads
		🦋	**#353** - Matte Dk. Cream 27 beads
		♣	**#052** - Lined Palest Peach AB 126 beads
		✳	**#323** - Matte Met. Purple Iris 97 beads
		♌	**#322** - Matte Met. Gold 131 beads
		☺	**#325** - Matte Met. Green Iris 123 beads
		★	**#310** - Matte Black 437 beads
		✋	**#233** - Lined Crystal Yellow Luster 38 beads
		●	**#380** - Matte Met. Green Pink 32 beads
		✤	**#084** - Lined Lt. Seafoam AB 136 beads
		✿	**#234** - Pale Pink Pearl 60 beads
		🐱	**#232** - Pale Yellow Pearl 70 beads
		✿	**#351** - Matte White 175 beads
		♀	**#851** - Matte Transp. Crystal AB 74 beads
		🐾	**#860** - Matte Transp. Green AB 56 beads
		🔑	**#876** - Matte Op. Green AB - 95 beads
		✂	**#301** - Matte Met. Blue Gray - 106 beads
		🐋	**#861** - Matte Lt. Blue AB 65 beads
		♟	**#871** - Matte Op. Oil Slick AB 268 beads
		→	**#882** - Matte Op. Sharkskin AB 71 beads
		🌷	**#126** - Pink Luster Lt. Olive 112 beads
		🚗	**#297** - Lined Ruby Black 64 beads
		♪	**#163** - Op. Green AB 23 beads
		🏮	**#003** - Green Iris 85 beads
		🎺	**#169** - Op. Neon Green AB 51 beads
		〰	**#327** - Matte Met. Teal Iris 113 beads

		♥	**#352** - Matte Cream 82 beads
		✳	**#884** - Matte Op. Chocolate AB 30 beads
		⬭	**#230** - 22 kt. Gold Lined 350 beads
		⬇	**#321** - Matte Met. Silver 63 beads
		◼	**#052** - Lined Palest Peach AB 27 beads
		♆	**#322** - Matte Met. Gold 10 beads
		⬅	**#325** - Matte Met. Green Iris 24 beads
		☯	**#310** - Matte Black 1046 beads
		◆	**#851** - Matte Transp. Crystal AB 97 beads
		🦋	**#860** - Matte Transp. Green AB 27 beads
		♣	**#871** - Matte Op. Oil Slick AB 62 beads
		✳	**#882** - Matte Op. Sharkskin AB 62 beads
		↺	**#003** - Green Iris 570 beads
		☺	**#169** - Op. Neon Green AB 30 beads
		☆	**#327** - Matte Met. Teal Iris 547 beads
		✋	**#373** - Matte Met. Leaf Green 98 beads
		⬭	**#690** - Semi Matte SL Dk. Gray Green 236 beads
		❖	**#853** - Matte Transp. Dk. Topaz AB 17 beads
		⚙	**#035** - Galvanized Silver 79 beads
		🐱	**#460** - Galvanized Rose Gold 15 beads
		◉	**#372** - Matte Met. Lt. Yellow 124 beads
		♀	**#371** - Matte Met. Olive Gold 14 beads
		🐾	**#158** - Op. Lavender AB 27 beads
		⚷	**#241** - Pale Lavender Pearl 167 beads
		✂	**#252** - Ceylon Gray 111 beads
		🐋	**#356** - Matte Lavender 16 beads
		♟	**#379** - Matte Met. Old Rose 14 beads
		➡	**#454** - Galvanized Lt. Purple 11 beads
		🌷	**#765** - Matte Transp. Lilac 21 beads
		🚗	**#080** - Lined Pale Lavender AB 133 beads
		♪	**#429** - Galvanized Pale Lavender 51 beads
		📯	**#463** - Galvanized Dk. Fuchsia 284 beads
		🎺	**#606** - SL Khaki 147 beads

Flowers are always a favorite. This delicate pattern is balanced by the heavily beaded green and purple fringe.

Tiny Orchids
Back of Stealth

Stitch: Peyote or Brick   **Size:** Approximately 3¾" x 4⅛"   **Beads Used:** Delica

For straps and embellishments, gather your own collection of beads, natural stones and crystals. Plan a design that makes the bag uniquely yours. Note: The bead quantities given do not include fringe and strap.

Bag by Suzanne Siegel, Kalispell, MT   ssiegel@cyberport.net
Iris Glass by Iris Glass Art   irisglassart@cox.net

Clown School

Stitch a bit of ocean view with this underwater Clown Fish pattern. Catch an ocean wave of aqua blue fringe. Check out the stunning fish tank view in this absolutely fabulous matching lampwork bead!

Stitch: Peyote or Brick   Size: Approximately 3¾" x 4⅛"   Beads Used: Delica

Begin Here - work Peyote Stitch beginning with this row. Work from left to right across the pattern.

For straps and embellishments, gather your own collection of beads, natural stones and crystals. Plan a design that makes the bag uniquely yours. Note: The bead quantities given do not include fringe and strap.

Bag by Toni Hrabak, Kamiah, Idaho
Fish Tank lampwork bead LandS Art

tonih@cybrquest.com
landsart.com

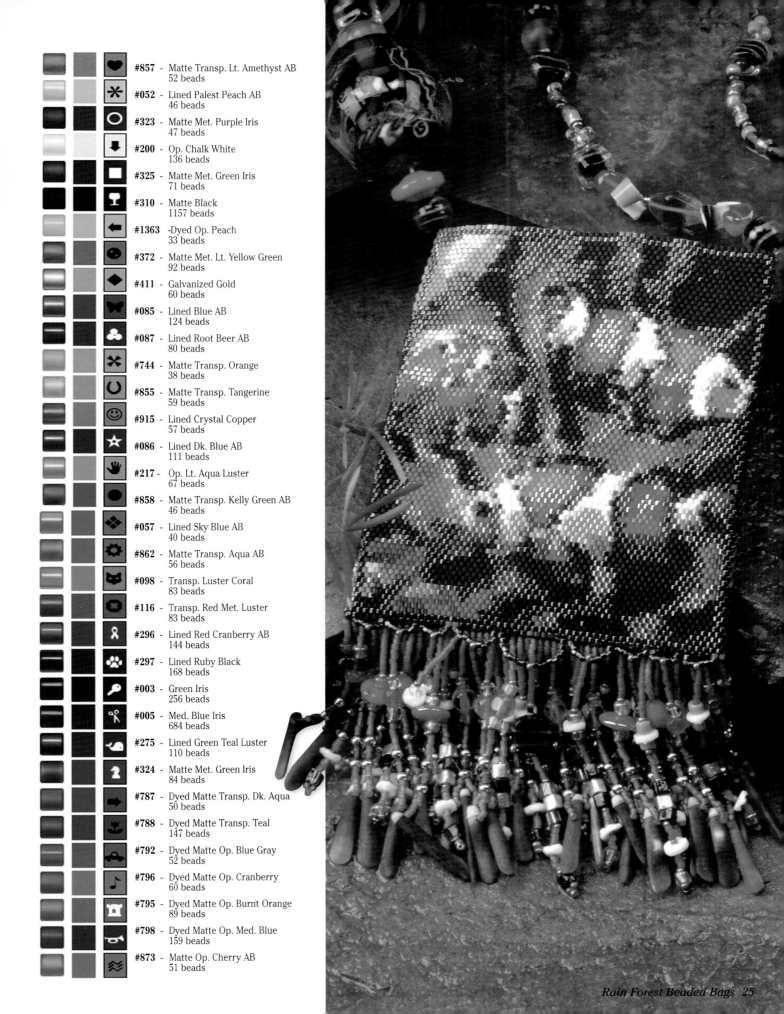

#857 - Matte Transp. Lt. Amethyst AB
52 beads

#052 - Lined Palest Peach AB
46 beads

#323 - Matte Met. Purple Iris
47 beads

#200 - Op. Chalk White
136 beads

#325 - Matte Met. Green Iris
71 beads

#310 - Matte Black
1157 beads

#1363 - Dyed Op. Peach
33 beads

#372 - Matte Met. Lt. Yellow Green
92 beads

#411 - Galvanized Gold
60 beads

#085 - Lined Blue AB
124 beads

#087 - Lined Root Beer AB
80 beads

#744 - Matte Transp. Orange
38 beads

#855 - Matte Transp. Tangerine
59 beads

#915 - Lined Crystal Copper
57 beads

#086 - Lined Dk. Blue AB
111 beads

#217 - Op. Lt. Aqua Luster
67 beads

#858 - Matte Transp. Kelly Green AB
46 beads

#057 - Lined Sky Blue AB
40 beads

#862 - Matte Transp. Aqua AB
56 beads

#098 - Transp. Luster Coral
83 beads

#116 - Transp. Red Met. Luster
83 beads

#296 - Lined Red Cranberry AB
144 beads

#297 - Lined Ruby Black
168 beads

#003 - Green Iris
256 beads

#005 - Med. Blue Iris
684 beads

#275 - Lined Green Teal Luster
110 beads

#324 - Matte Met. Green Iris
84 beads

#787 - Dyed Matte Transp. Dk. Aqua
50 beads

#788 - Dyed Matte Transp. Teal
147 beads

#792 - Dyed Matte Op. Blue Gray
52 beads

#796 - Dyed Matte Op. Cranberry
60 beads

#795 - Dyed Matte Op. Burnt Orange
89 beads

#798 - Dyed Matte Op. Med. Blue
159 beads

#873 - Matte Op. Cherry AB
51 beads

#200 - Op. Chalk White
320 beads

#411 - Galvanized Gold
510 beads

#087 - Lined Root Beer
108 beads

#744 - Matte Transp. Orange
132 beads

#915 - Lined Crystal Copper
206 beads

#862 - Matte Transp. Aqua AB
2324 beads

#005 - Medium Blue Iris
384 beads

#873 - Matte Op. Cherry AB
608 beads

Clown School

Using the same colors as the Clown School, create a bold geometric with a Southwest desert feel. Here the same blue that created "water" now evokes a sense of endless sky.

Stitch: Peyote or Brick   **Size:** Approximately 3¾" x 4⅛"   **Beads Used:** Delica

Begin Here - work Peyote Stitch beginning with this row. Work from left to right across the pattern.

For straps and embellishments, gather your own collection of beads, natural stones and crystals. Plan a design that makes the bag uniquely yours. Note: The bead quantities given do not include fringe and strap.

Bag by Toni Hrabak, Kamiah, Idaho   tonih@cybrquest.com
Fish Tank lampwork bead LandS Art   landsart.com

Red Panda

Someone's watching from a limb above. Stitch this sweet face in a natural green habitat for a beautiful bag, or applique the finished piece to a shirt or vest. You're sure to attract some second looks when you wear this friendly panda.

Stitch: Peyote or Brick   Size: Approximately 3¾" x 4⅛"   Beads Used: Delica

Begin Here - work Peyote Stitch beginning with this row. Work from left to right across the pattern.

For straps and embellishments, gather your own collection of beads, natural stones and crystals. Plan a design that makes the bag uniquely yours. Note: The bead quantities given do not include fringe and strap.

Bag by Val Jensen, Boise, Idaho   vjensen@emeraldtran.com
Glass beads - Two Sisters Designs twosisters1.freeservers.com

		Symbol	#	Name	Beads
		♥	#203	Ceylon Lt. Yellow	251 beads
		✳	#204	Ceylon Lt. Blue	70 beads
		○	#205	Ceylon Beige	27 beads
		▼	#853	Matte Transp. Dk. Topaz AB	174 beads
		■	#857	Matte Transp. Lt. Amethyst AB	74 beads
		♒	#863	Matte Transp. Shark Gray AB	126 beads
		←	#884	Matte Op. Chocolate AB	38 beads
		◉	#321	Matte Met. Silver	77 beads
		◆	#052	Lined Palest Peach AB	219 beads
		✖	#323	Matte Met. Purple Iris	93 beads
		♣	#287	Lined Topaz Amber	154 beads
		✳	#325	Matte Met. Blue Iris	25 beads
		↺	#310	Matte Black	210 beads
		☺	#380	Matte Met. Green Pink	23 beads
		★	#372	Matte Met. Lt. Yellow Green	196 beads
		✋	#232	Pale Yellow Pearl	36 beads
		●	#351	Matte White	185 beads
		◈	#860	Matte Transp. Green AB	115 beads
		⚙	#876	Matte Op. Green AB	208 beads
		🐱	#871	Matte Op. Oil Slick AB	38 beads
		◉	#061	Lined Wine AB	158 beads
		♀	#865	Matte Transp. Dk. Chocolate AB	108 beads
		🐾	#087	Lined Root Beer AB	262 beads
		🔑	#180	Transp. Brown AB	136 beads
		✂	#312	Matte Met. Copper	64 beads
		🐋	#794	Dyed Matte Op. Chestnut	241 beads
		♞	#023	Met. Lt. Bronze Iris	278 beads
		→	#129	Pink Luster Topaz	159 beads
		🌷	#297	Lined Ruby Black	165 beads
		🚗	#060	Lined Lime AB	52 beads
		♪	#273	Lined Topaz Olive AB	87 beads
		🎀	#069	Lined Beige AB	197 beads
		🎺	#054	Lined Peach AB	32 beads
		〰	#764	Matte Transp. Chestnut Brown	128 beads
		★	#769	Matte Transp. Chocolate Brown	186 beads

#203 - Ceylon Lt. Yellow
18 beads

#052 - Lined Palest Peach AB
239 beads

#232 - Pale Yellow Pearl
84 beads

#351 - Matte White
427 beads

#860 - Matte Transp. Green AB
20 beads

#876 - Matte Op. Green AB
300 beads

#865 - Matte Transp. Dk. Chocolate AB
2245 beads

#023 - Met. Lt. Bronze Iris
959 beads

#060 - Lined Lime AB
54 beads

#273 - Lined Topaz Olive AB
138 beads

#054 - Lined Peach AB
108 beads

This geometric is so elegant, worked in rose and green beads. Add a touch of Victorian elegance with glass beads on the fringe.

Stitch: Peyote or Brick   Size: Approximately 3¾" x 4⅛"   Beads Used: Delica

Begin Here - work Peyote Stitch beginning with this row. Work from left to right across the pattern.

For straps and embellishments, gather your own collection of beads, natural stones and crystals. Plan a design that makes the bag uniquely yours. Note: The bead quantities given do not include fringe and strap.

Bag by Val Jensen, Boise, Idaho   vjensen@emeraldtran.com
Glass beads - Two Sisters Designs twosisters1.freeservers.com

		♥	#204 -	Ceylon Lt. Beige 392 beads
		✳	#207 -	Op. Peach Luster 45 beads
		⬭	#420 -	Galvanized Pink 306 beads
		⬇	#310 -	Matte Black 2331 beads
		⬛	#1363 -	-Dyed Op. Peach 18 beads
		♟	#146 -	SL Lt. Lavender 27 beads
		⬅	#234 -	Pale Pink Pearl 77 beads
		◉	#351 -	Matte White 352 beads
		◆	#912 -	Lined Crystal Taupe 54 beads
		🦋	#110 -	Transp. Lt. Blue AB 31 beads
		♣	#239 -	Lt. Aqua Pearl 13 beads
		✳	#055 -	Lined Pale Pink 74 beads
		⎈	#061 -	Lined Wine AB 14 beads
		☺	#257 -	Pale Blue Pearl 19 beads
		★	#419 -	Galvanized Dk. Rose 59 beads
		✋	#126 -	Pink Luster Lt. Olive 46 beads
		●	#915 -	Lined Crystal Copper 16 beads
		❖	#105 -	Gold Luster Dk. Red 14 beads
		⚙	#106 -	Transp. Pink Luster 28 beads
		🐱	#296 -	Lined Cranberry AB 14 beads
		✪	#297 -	Lined Ruby Black 30 beads
		🎗	#753 -	Matte Op. Dk. Red 333 beads
		🐾	#743 -	Matte Transp. Yellow 24 beads
		🔑	#230 -	22 kt. Gold Lined 43 beads
		✂	#232 -	Pale Yellow Pearl 91 beads
		🐋	#233 -	Lined Crystal Yellow Luster 51 beads
		♘	#060 -	Lined Lime AB 11 beads
		➡	#372 -	Matte Met. Lt. Yellow Green 15 beads
		🌷	#794 -	Dyed Matte Op. Chestnut 19 beads
		🚗	#884 -	Matte Op. Chocolate AB 33 beads
		♪	#272 -	Lined Topaz Yellow AB 12 beads

If you love tropical flowers, this is the project for you! This one has a simple pattern, but the delicate shading is very life-like.

Phalenopsis Orchid

Stitch: Peyote or Brick   Size: Approximately 3¾" x 4⅛"   Beads Used: Delica

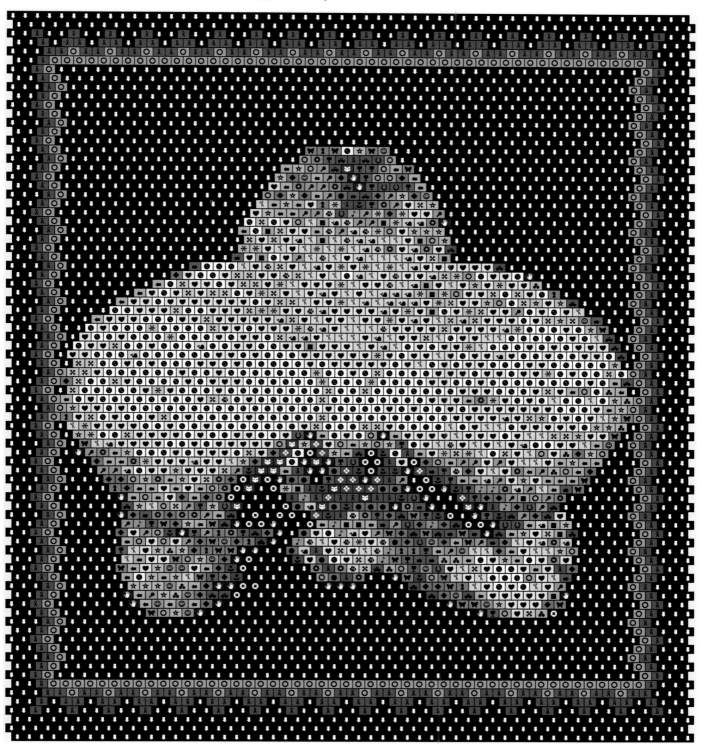

this row. Work from left to right across the pattern.

For straps and embellishments, gather your own collection of beads, natural stones and crystals. Plan a design that makes the bag uniquely yours. Note: The bead quantities given do not include fringe and strap.

Bag by Deb Atkins, The Bead Hive, Wichita, KS   D7442039@aol.com
Blass by Cindy, Blue Flame Art   BlueFlameArt@aol.com

Dragonfly
Back of Orchid

Bead a dazzling dragonfly against a silver blue sky. This wonderful beaded bag really shines when the light hits it, and so wil you when you wear it. Take a look at the gorgeous dragonfly lamp work bead at the bottom, and check out that sky blue fringe!

Stitch: Peyote or Brick   **Size:** Approximately 3¾" x 4⅛"   **Beads Used:** Delica

Begin Here - work Peyote Stitch beginning with this row. Work from left to right across the pattern.

For straps and embellishments, gather your own collection of beads, natural stones and crystals. Plan a design that makes the bag uniquely yours. Note: The bead quantities given do not include fringe and strap.

Bag by Deb Atkins, The Bead Hive, Wichita, KS   D7442039@aol.com
Blass by Cindy, Blue Flame Art   BlueFlameArt@aol.com